FEMININE WILD

ADULT COLORING BOOK

ORIGINAL ART BY ALISA BURKE & ANDY GUNTHARDT

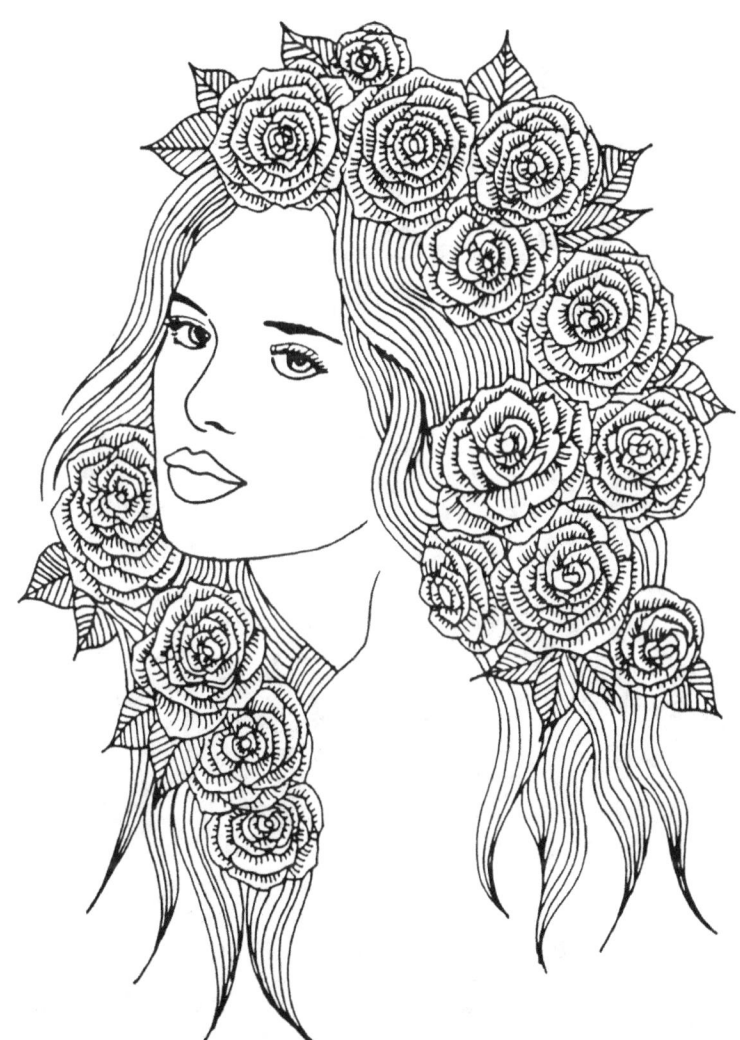

Here's to strong women. May we know them. May we be them. May we raise them.

—unknown

Feminine Wild Coloring Book
© 2016 Alisa Burke

www.alisaburke.com

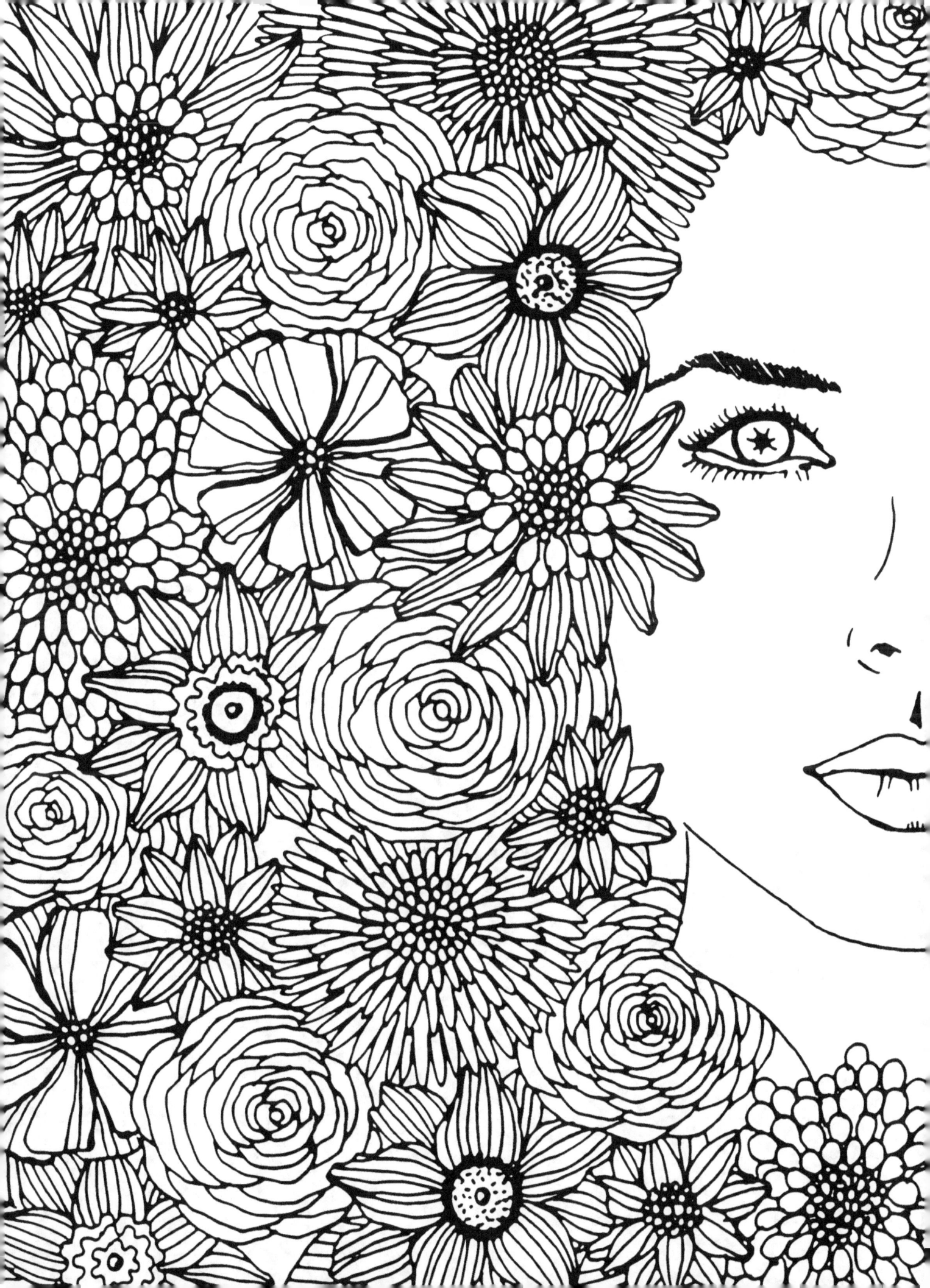

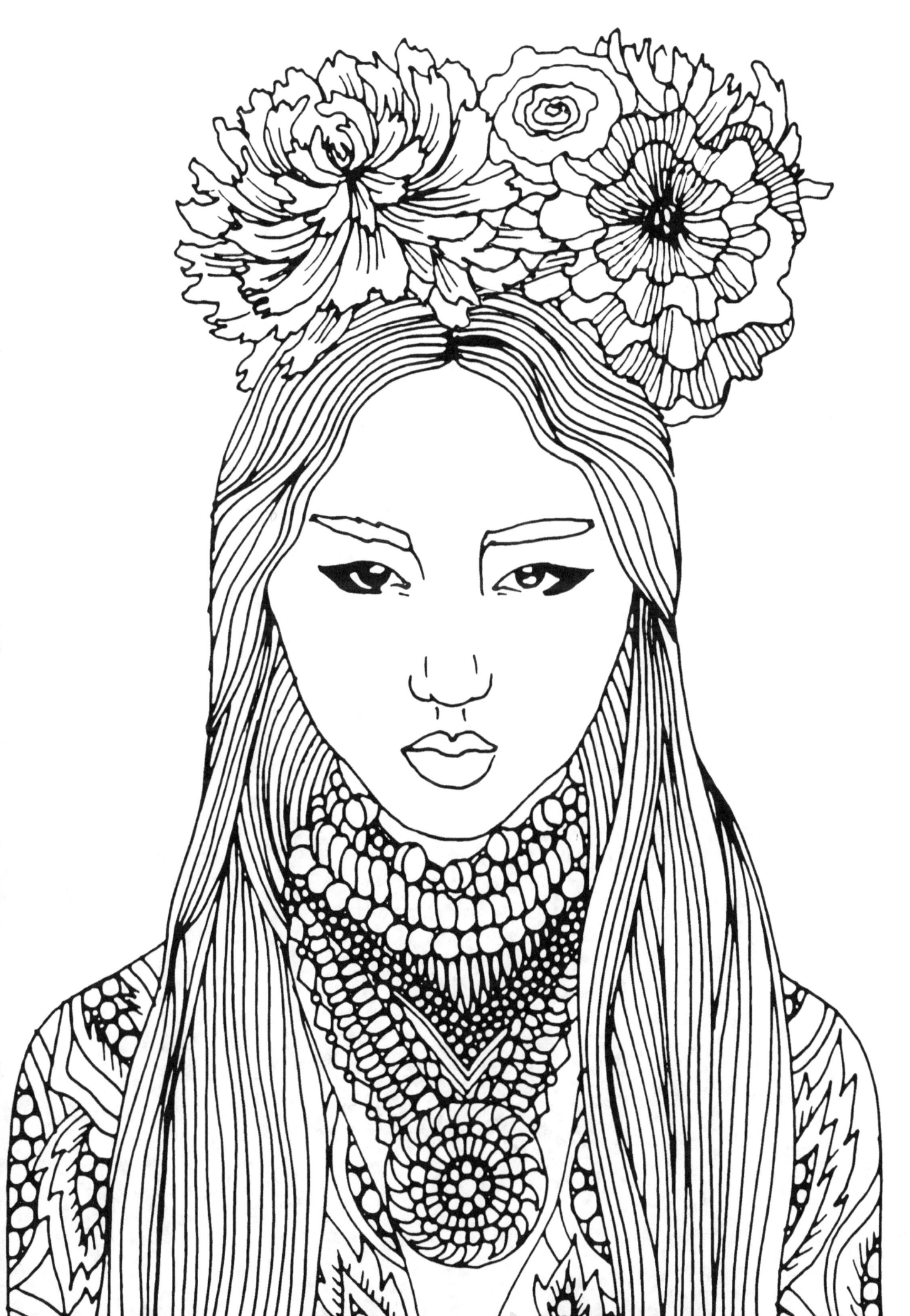

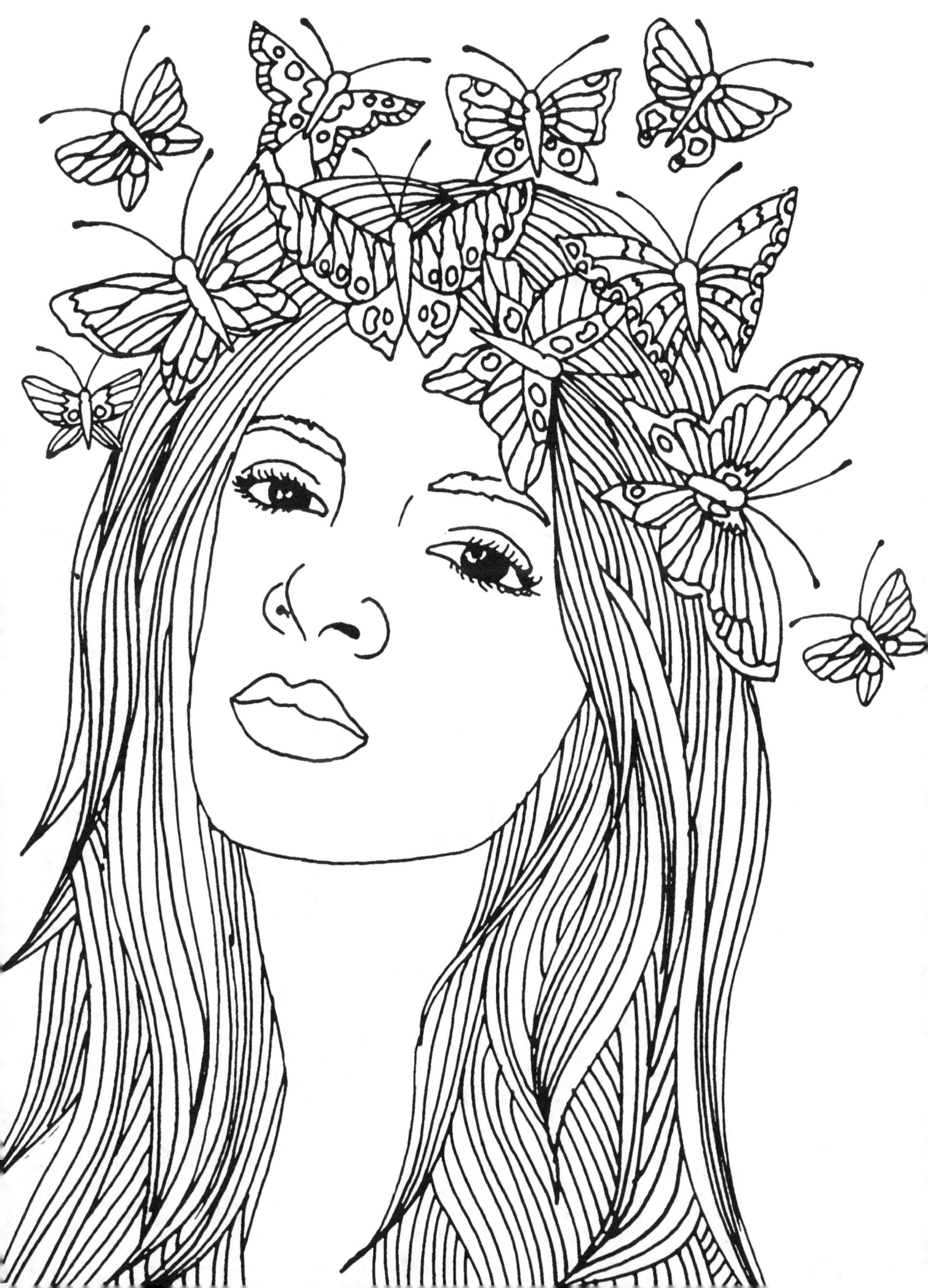

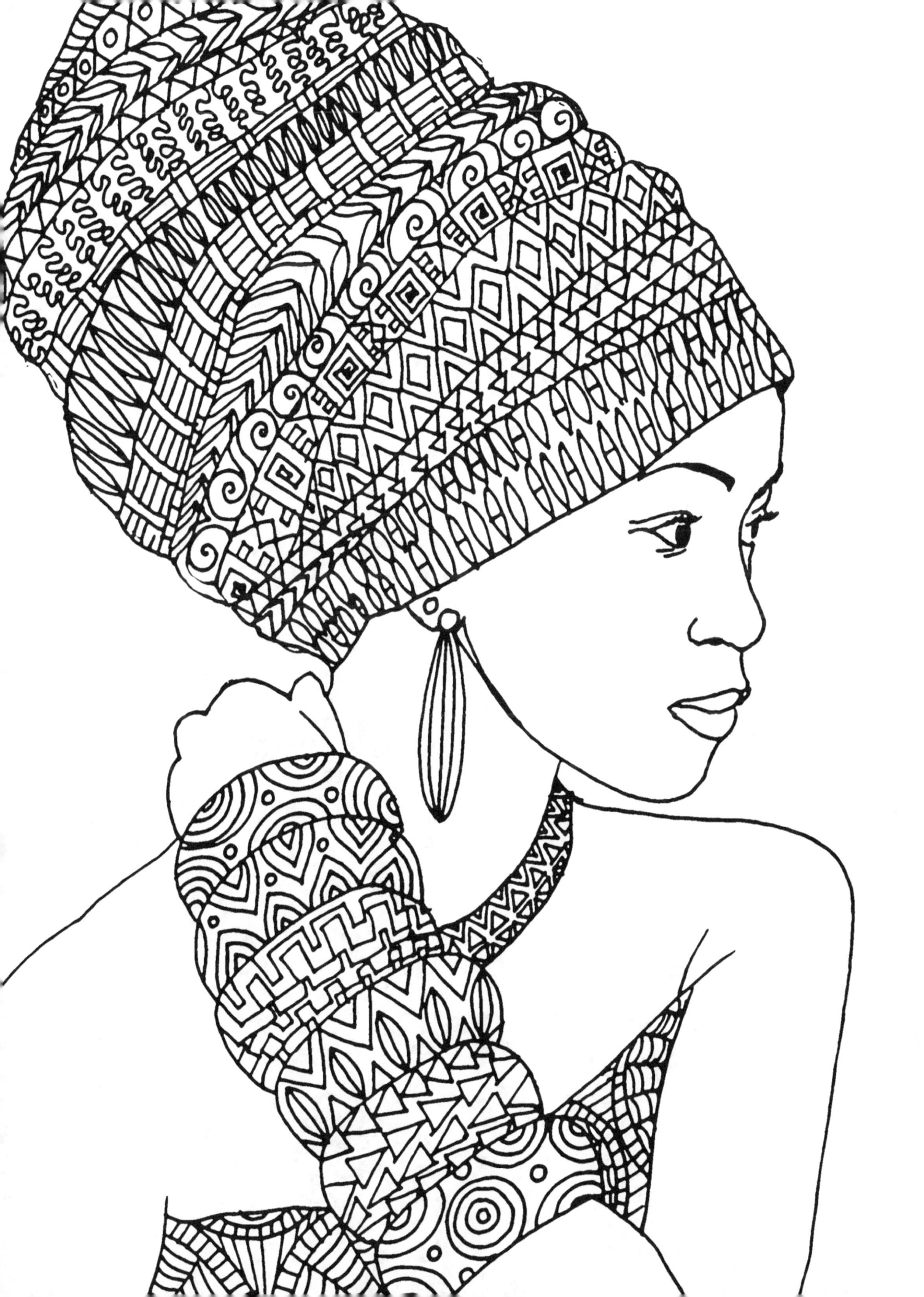

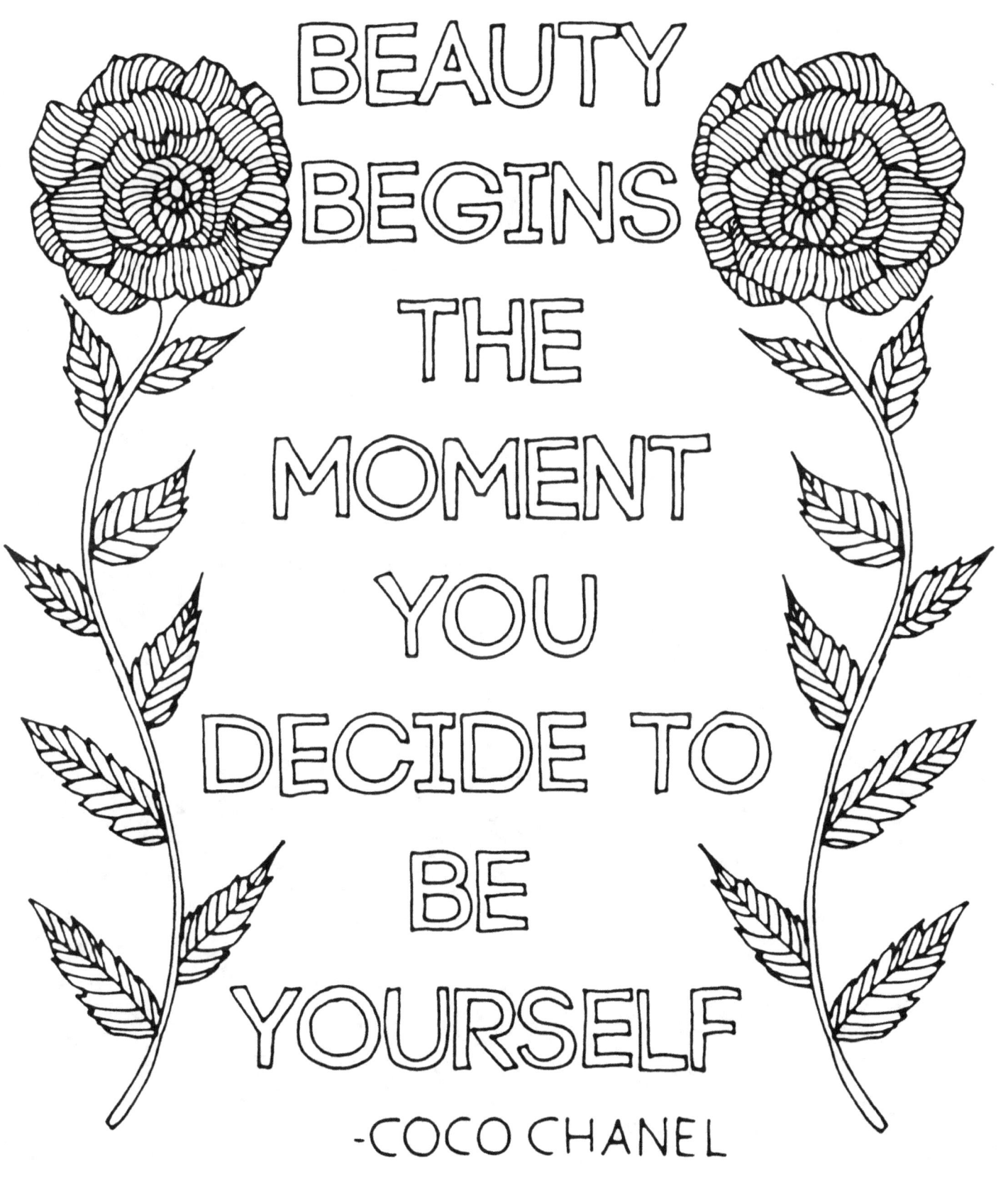

BEAUTY BEGINS THE MOMENT YOU DECIDE TO BE YOURSELF

-COCO CHANEL

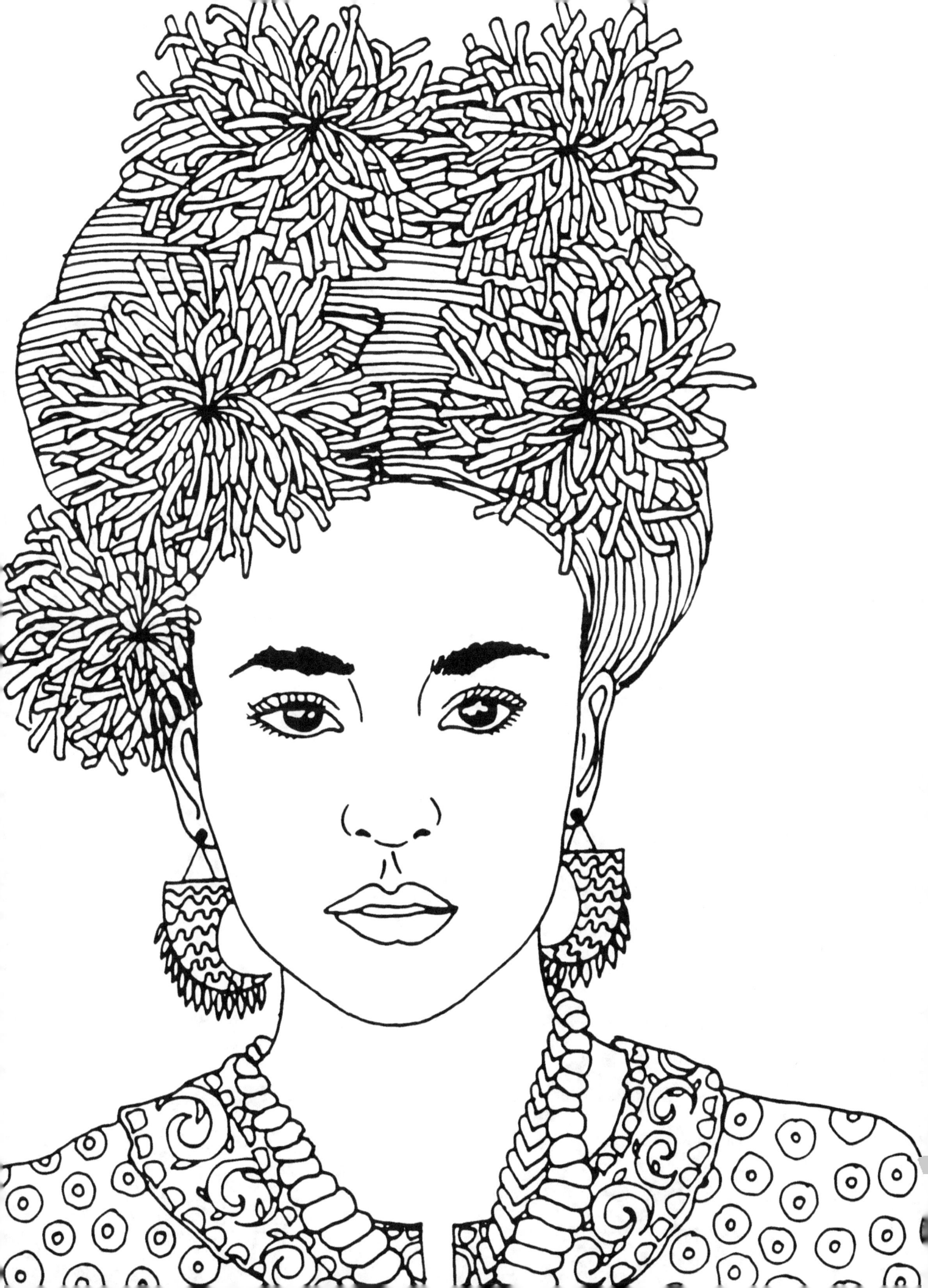

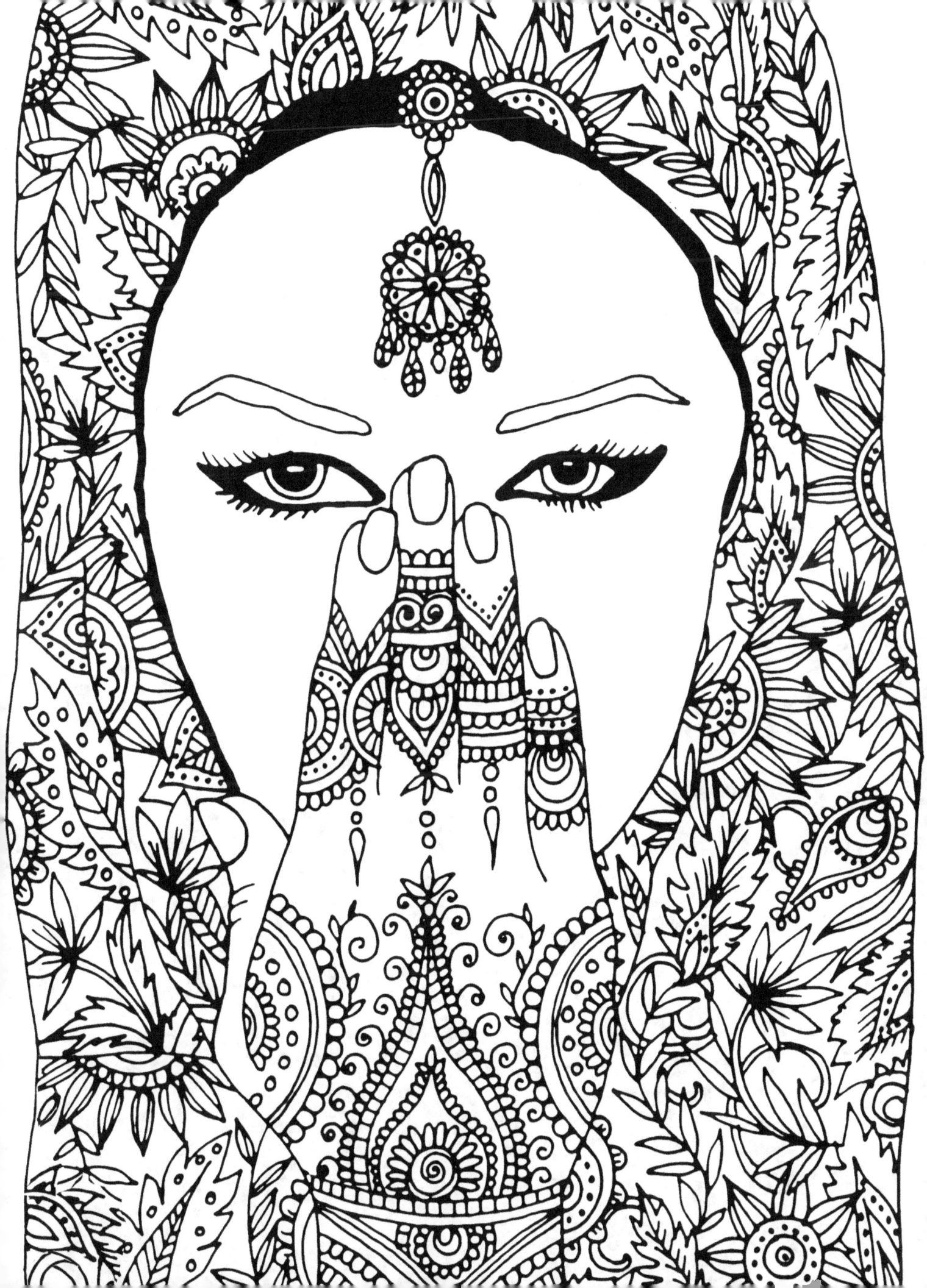

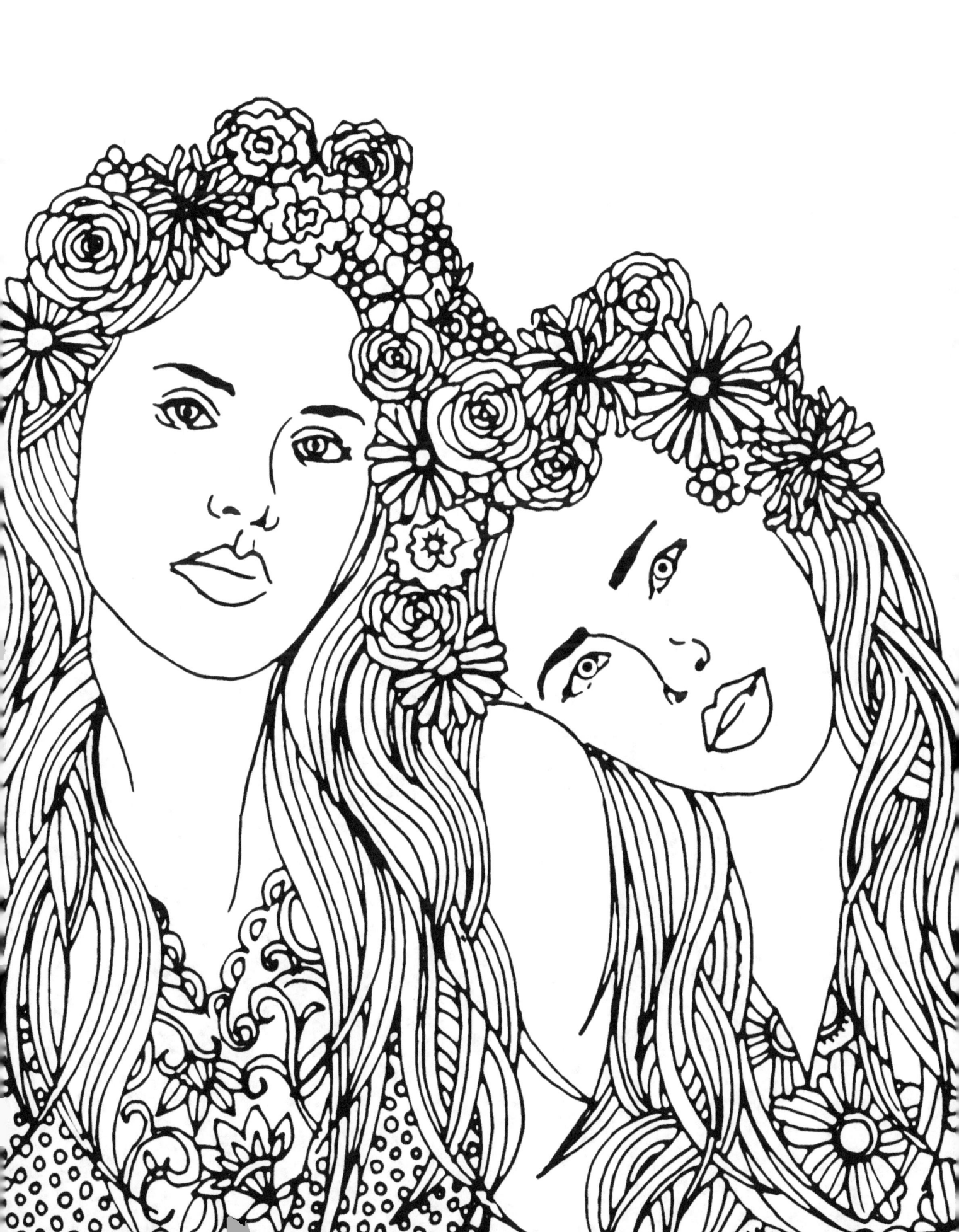

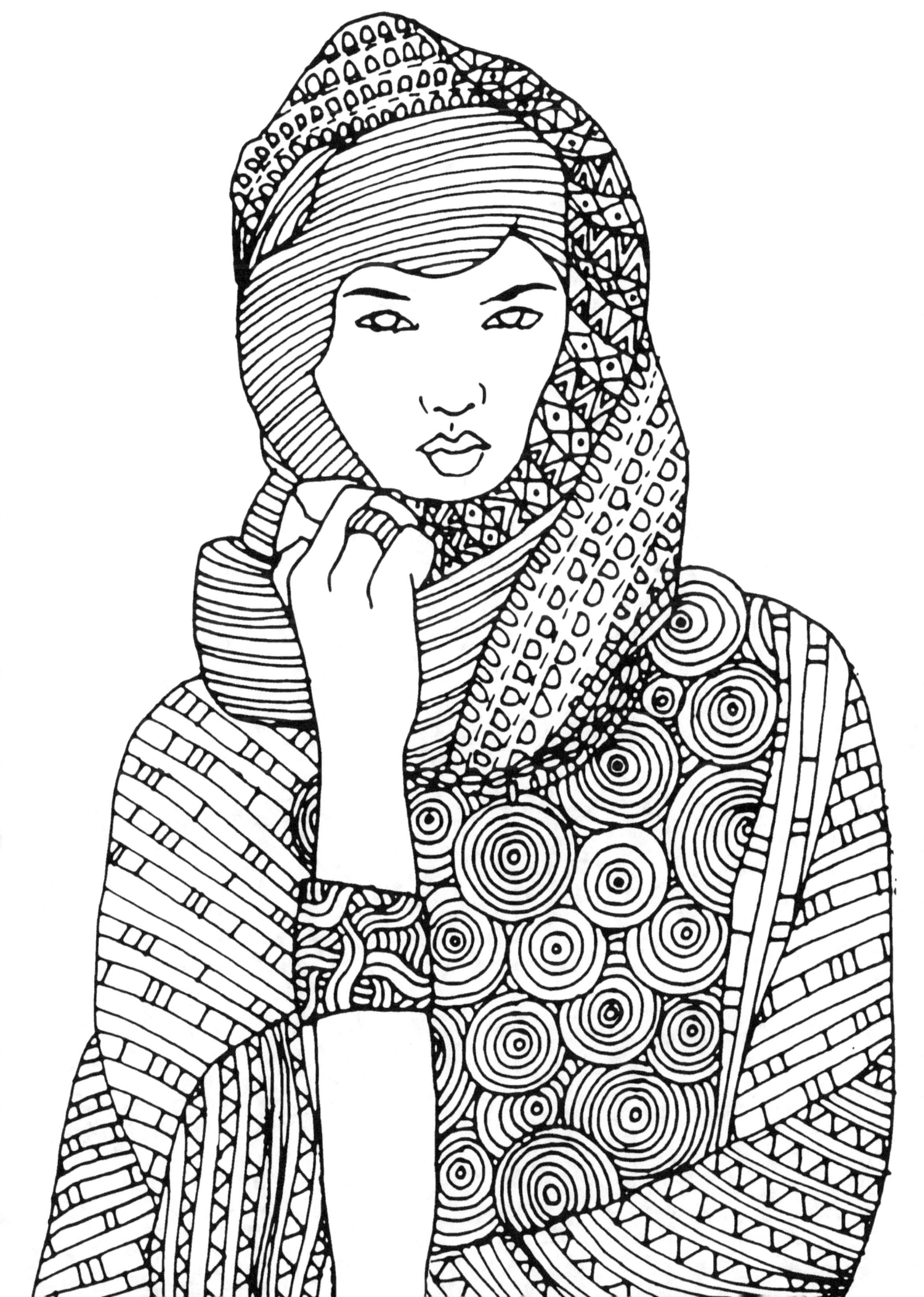

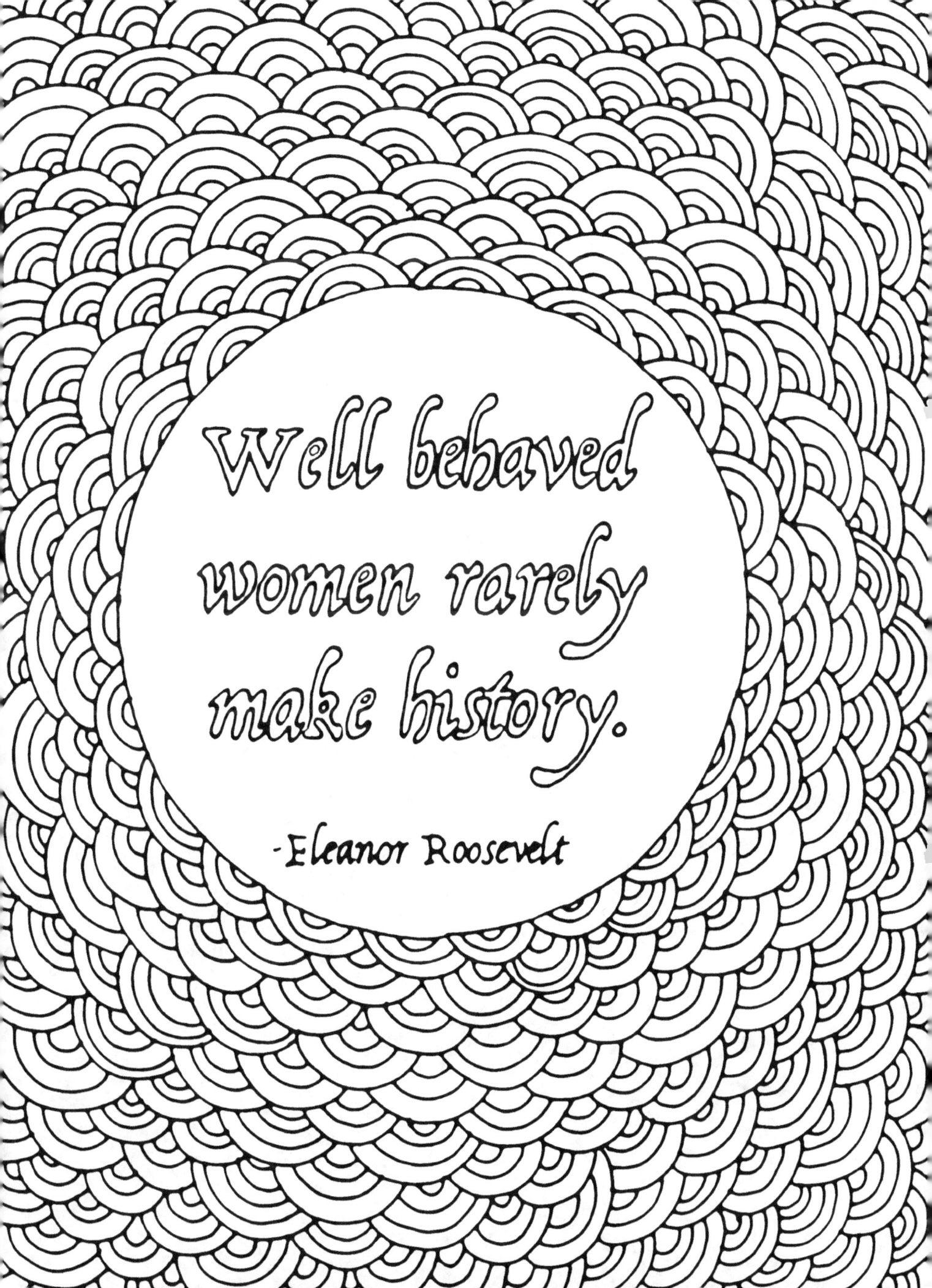

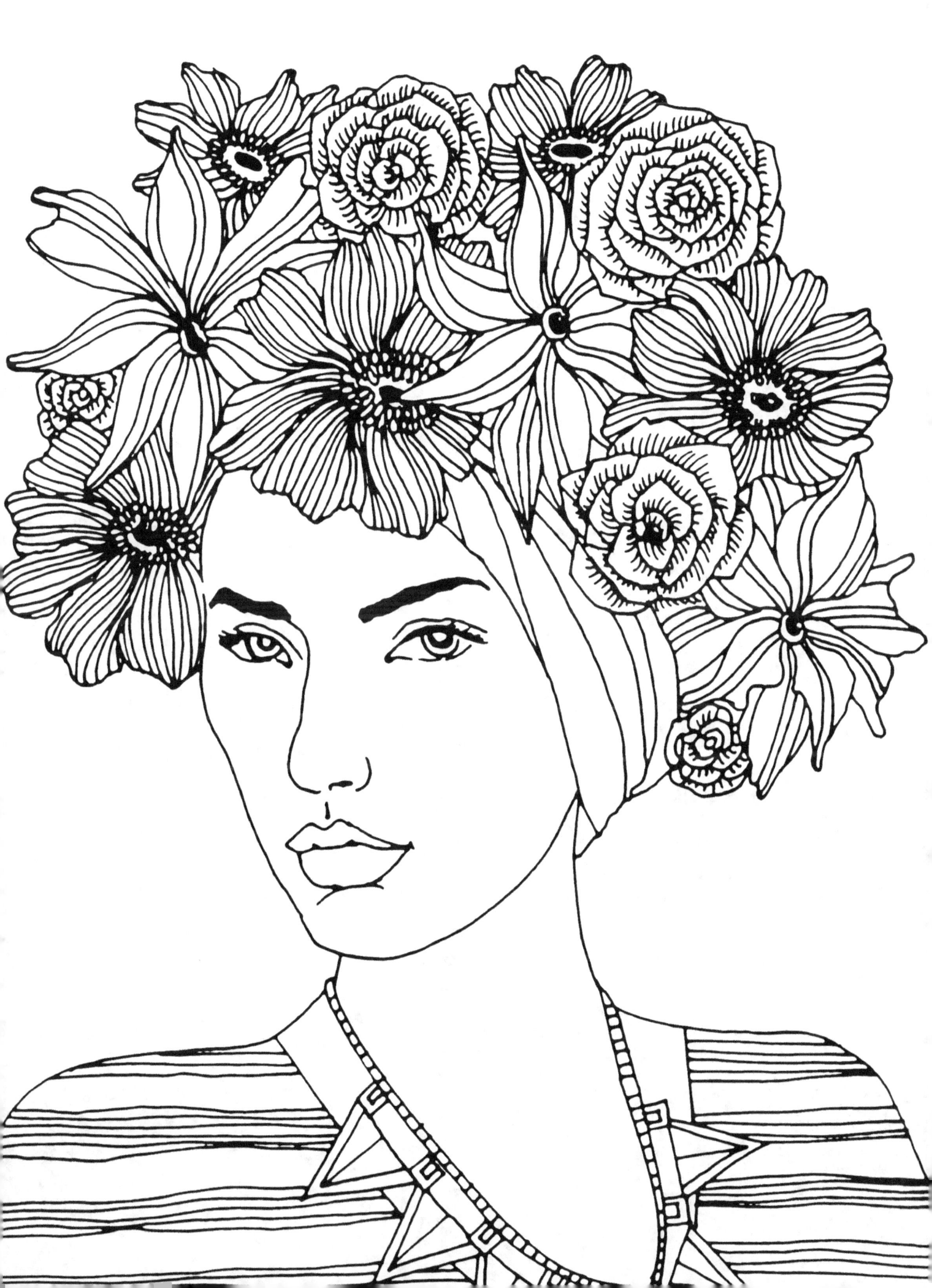

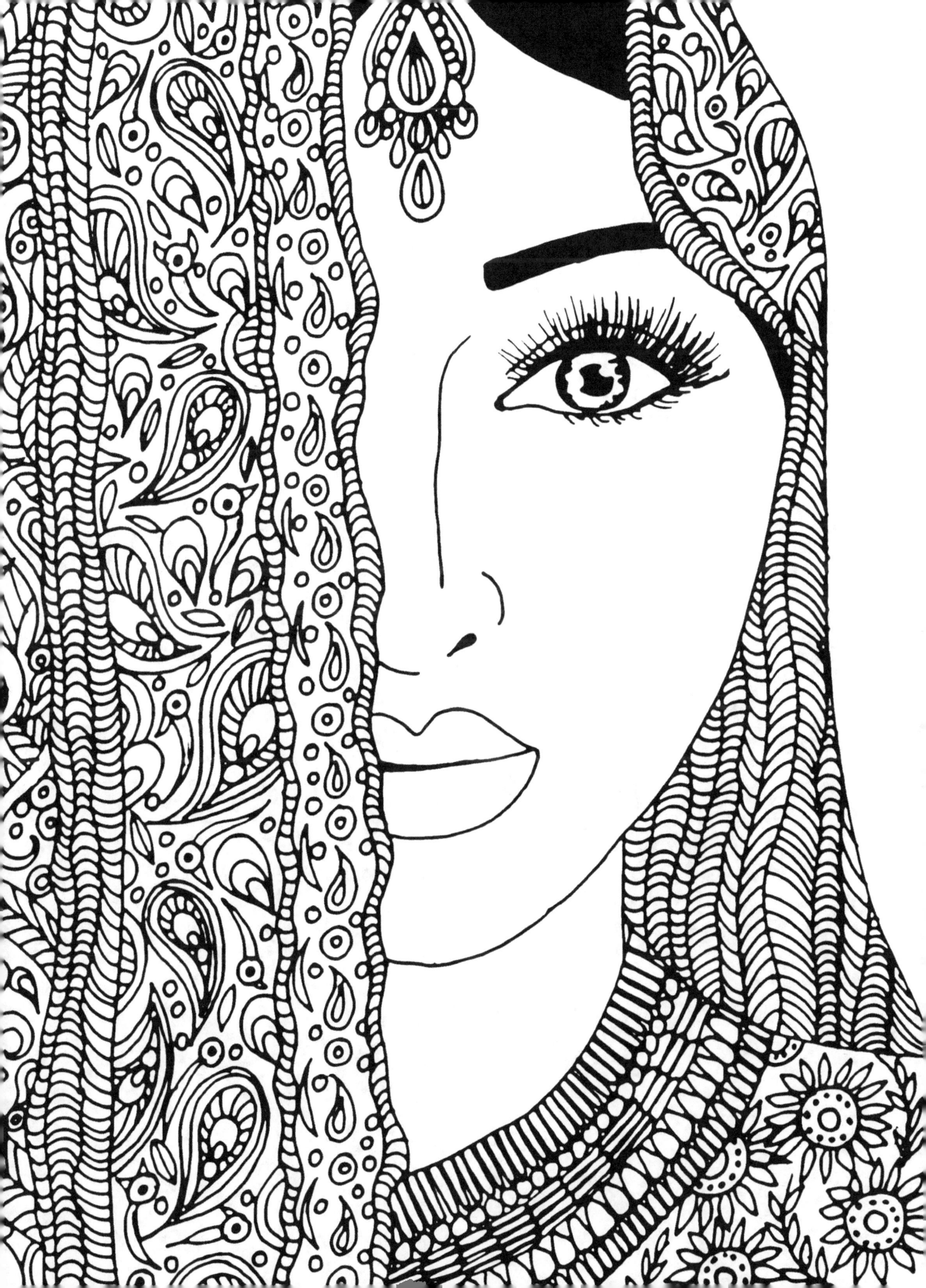

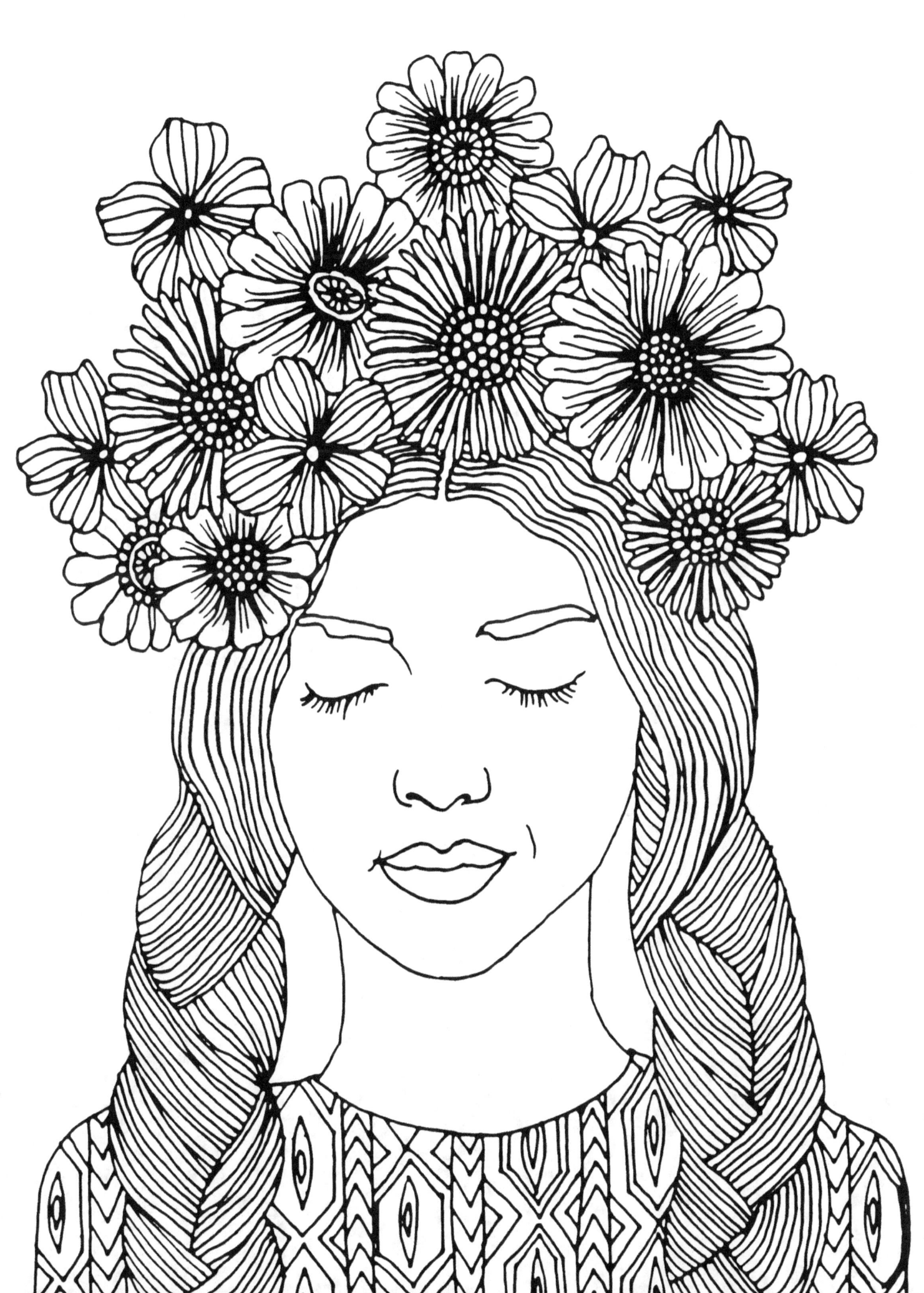

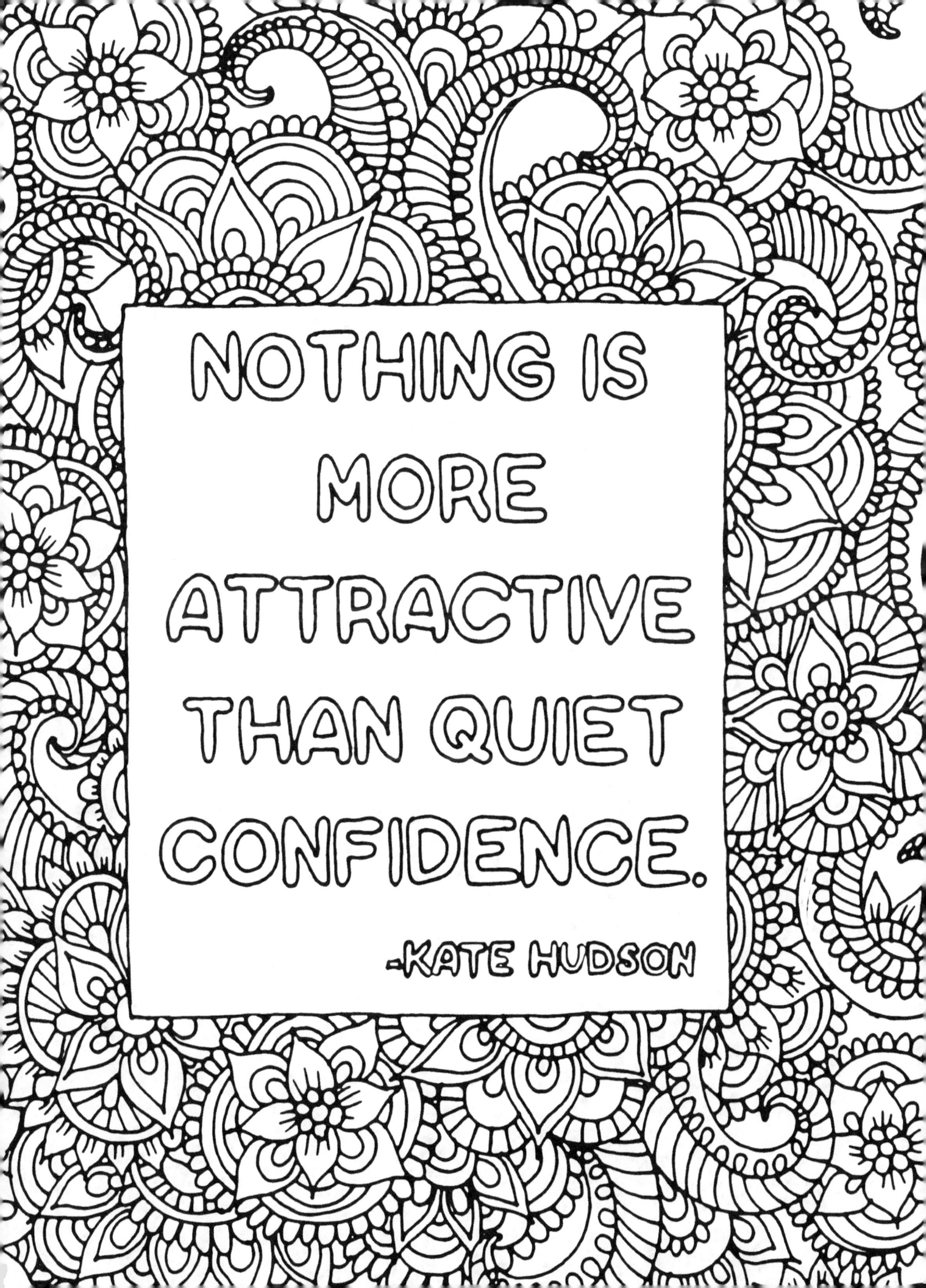

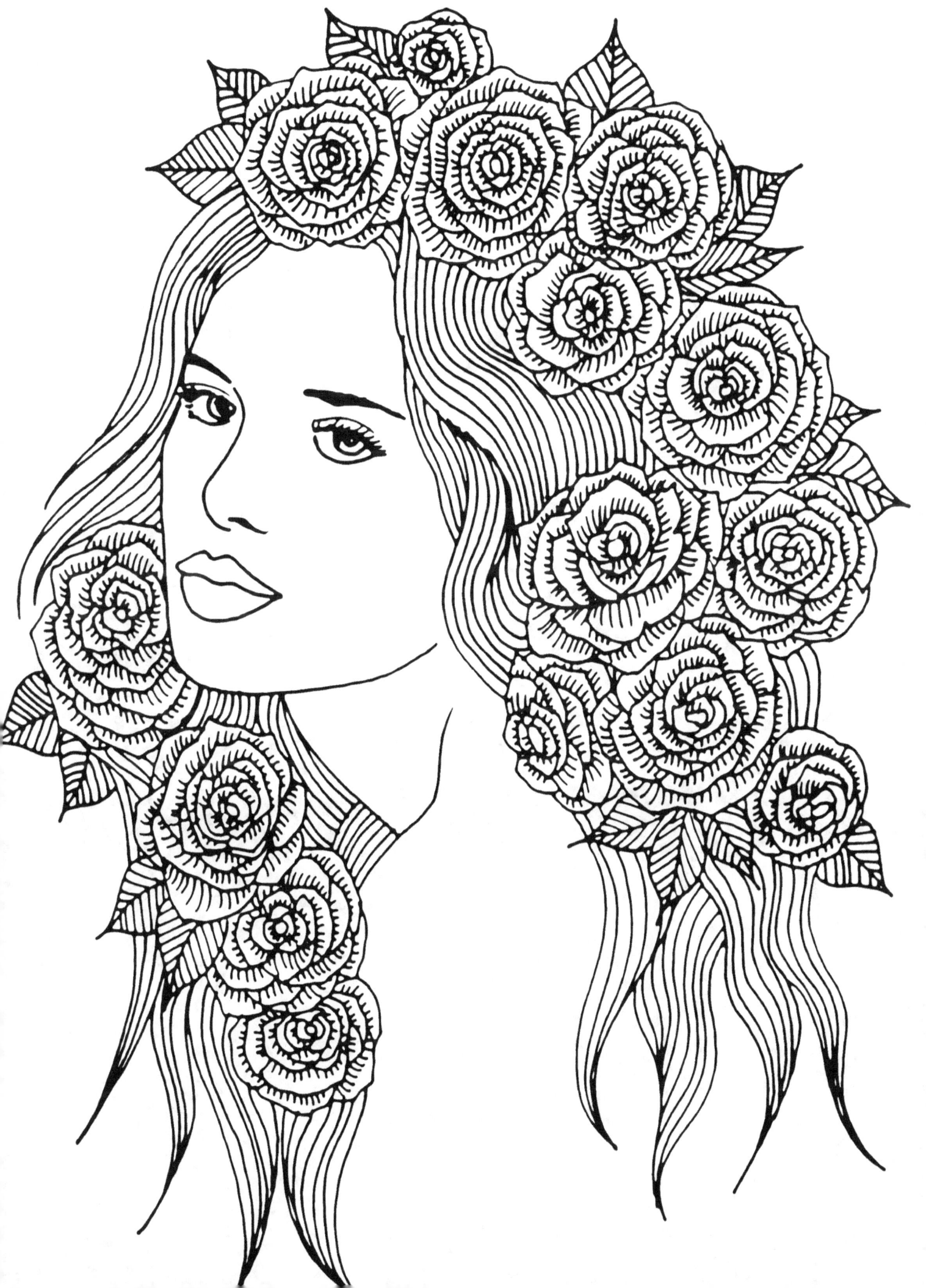

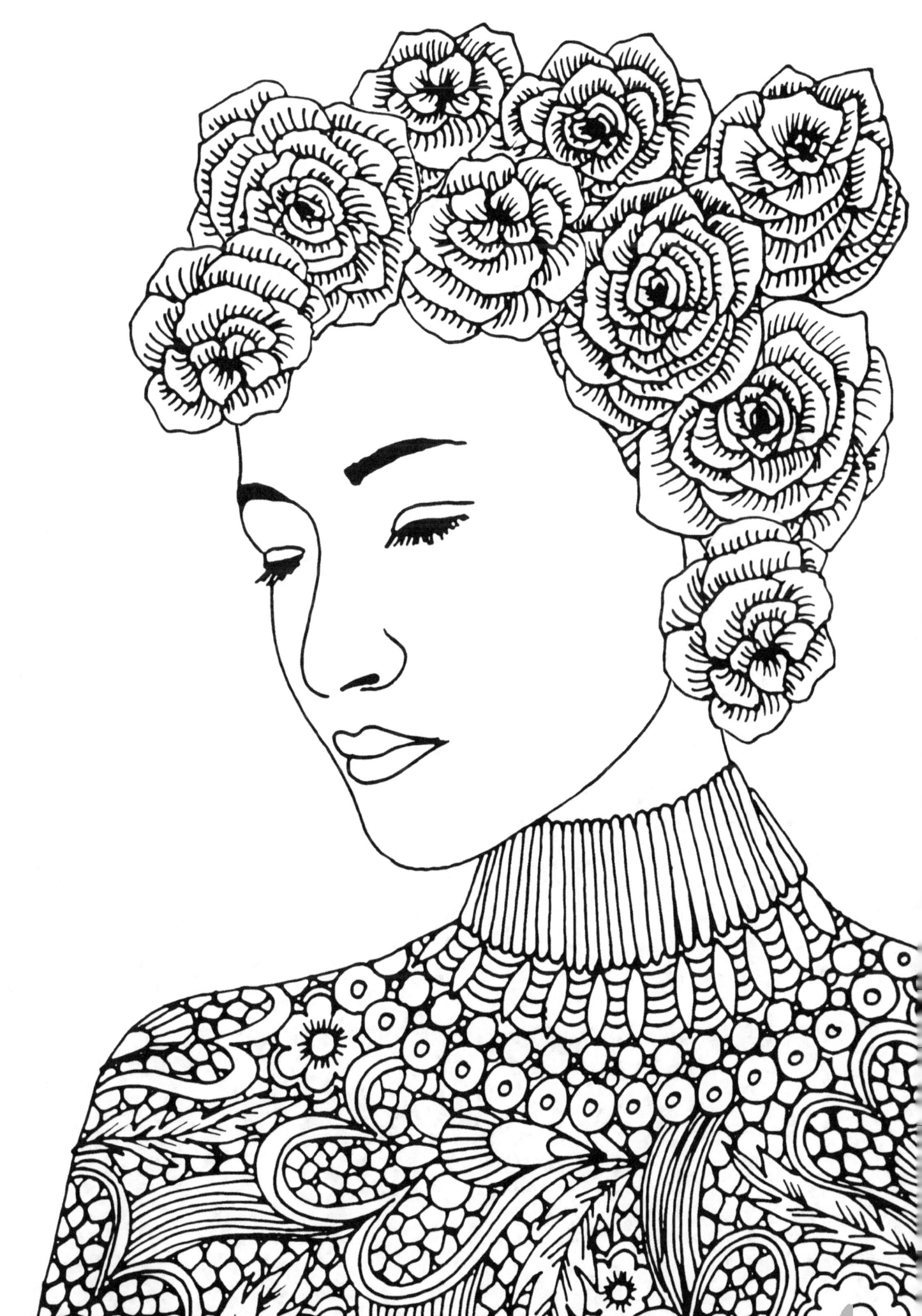

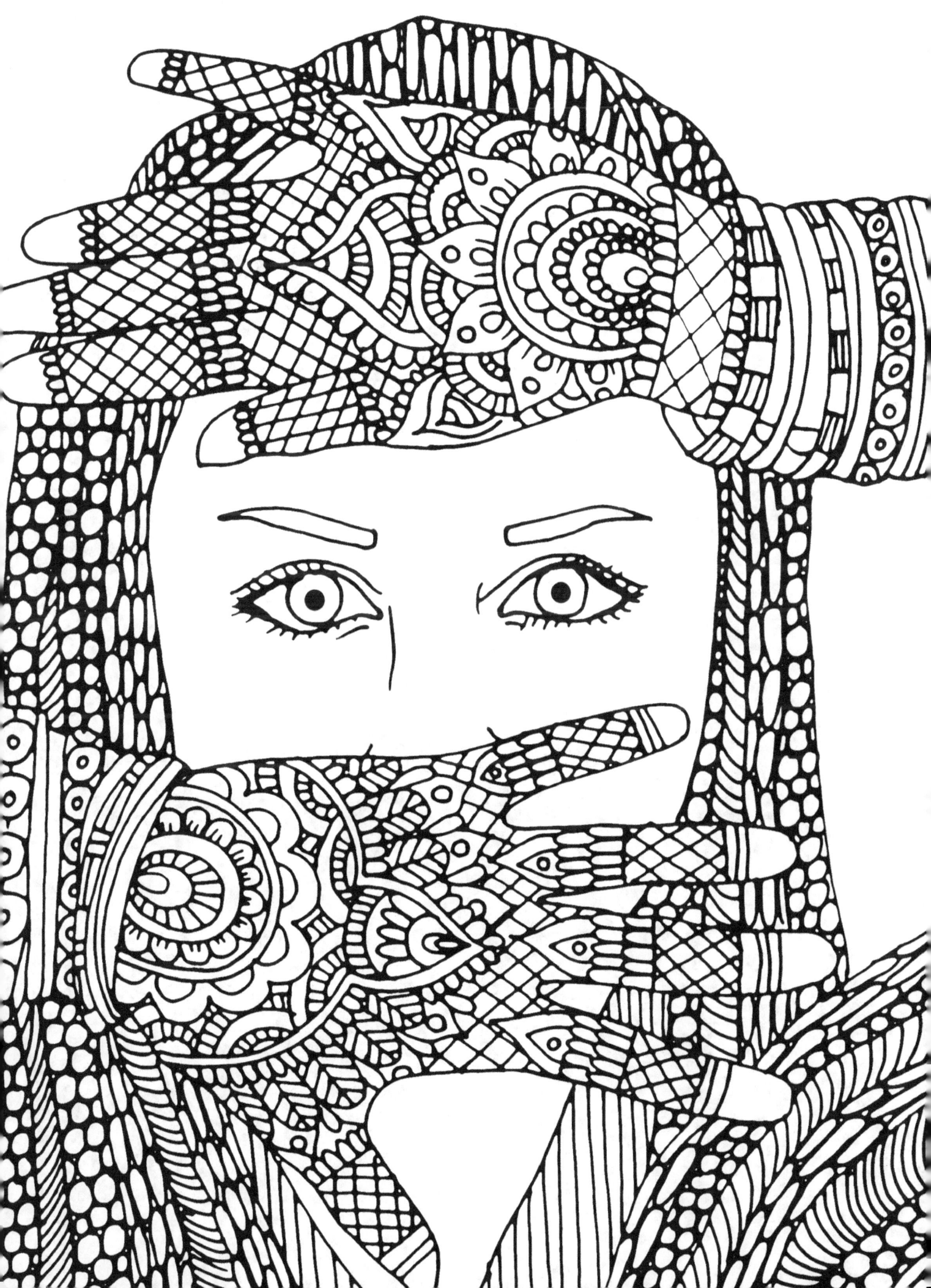

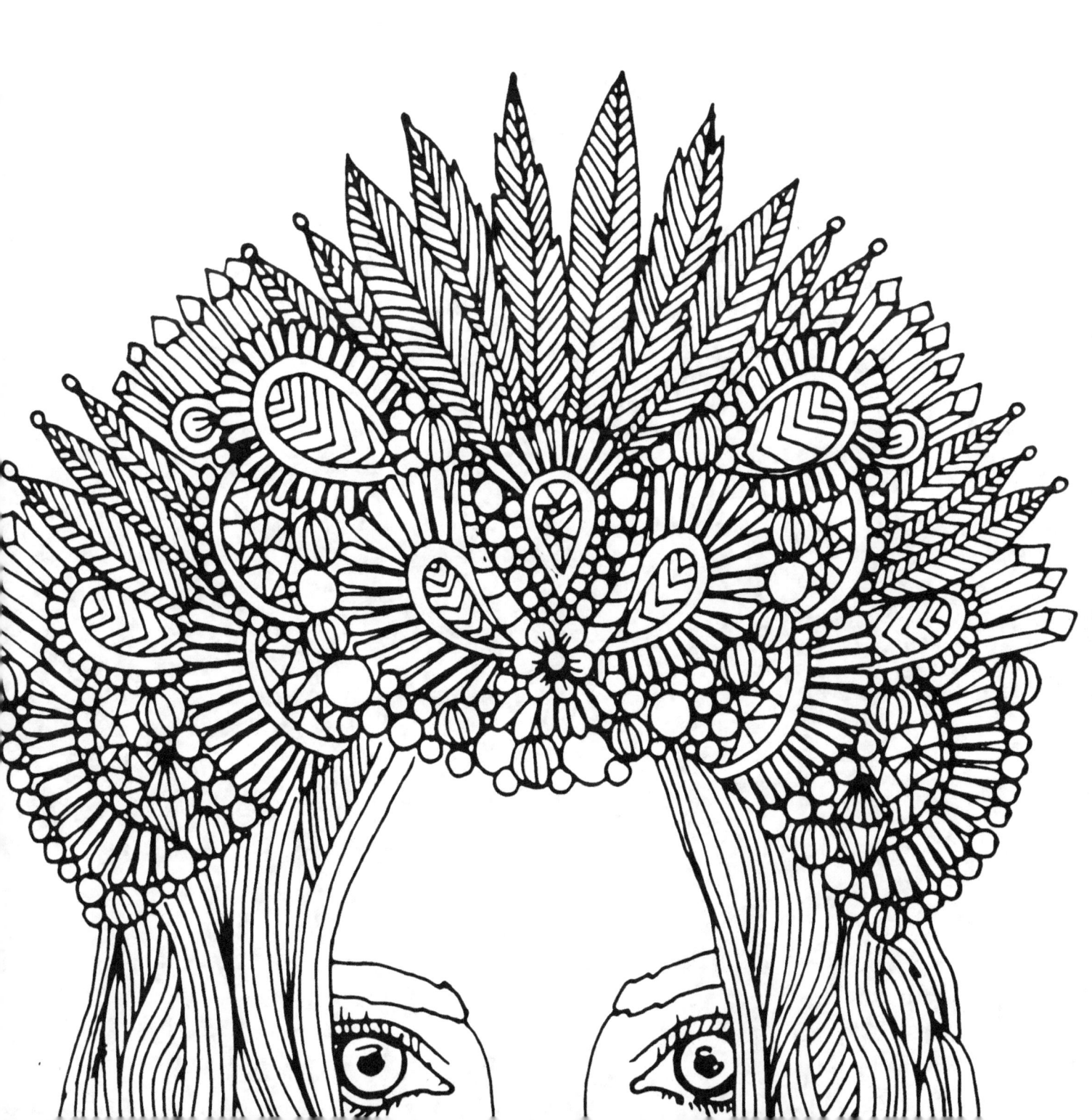

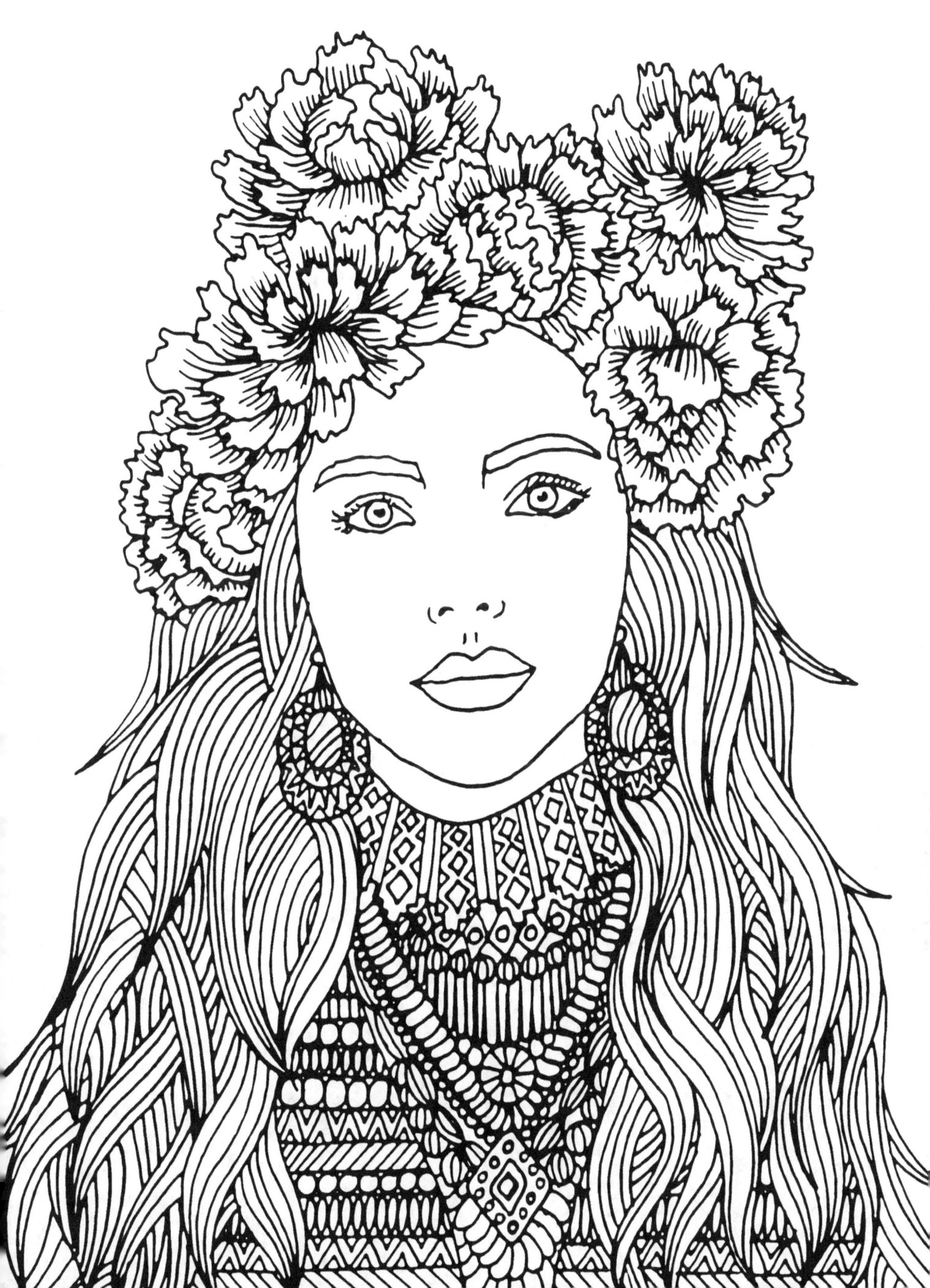

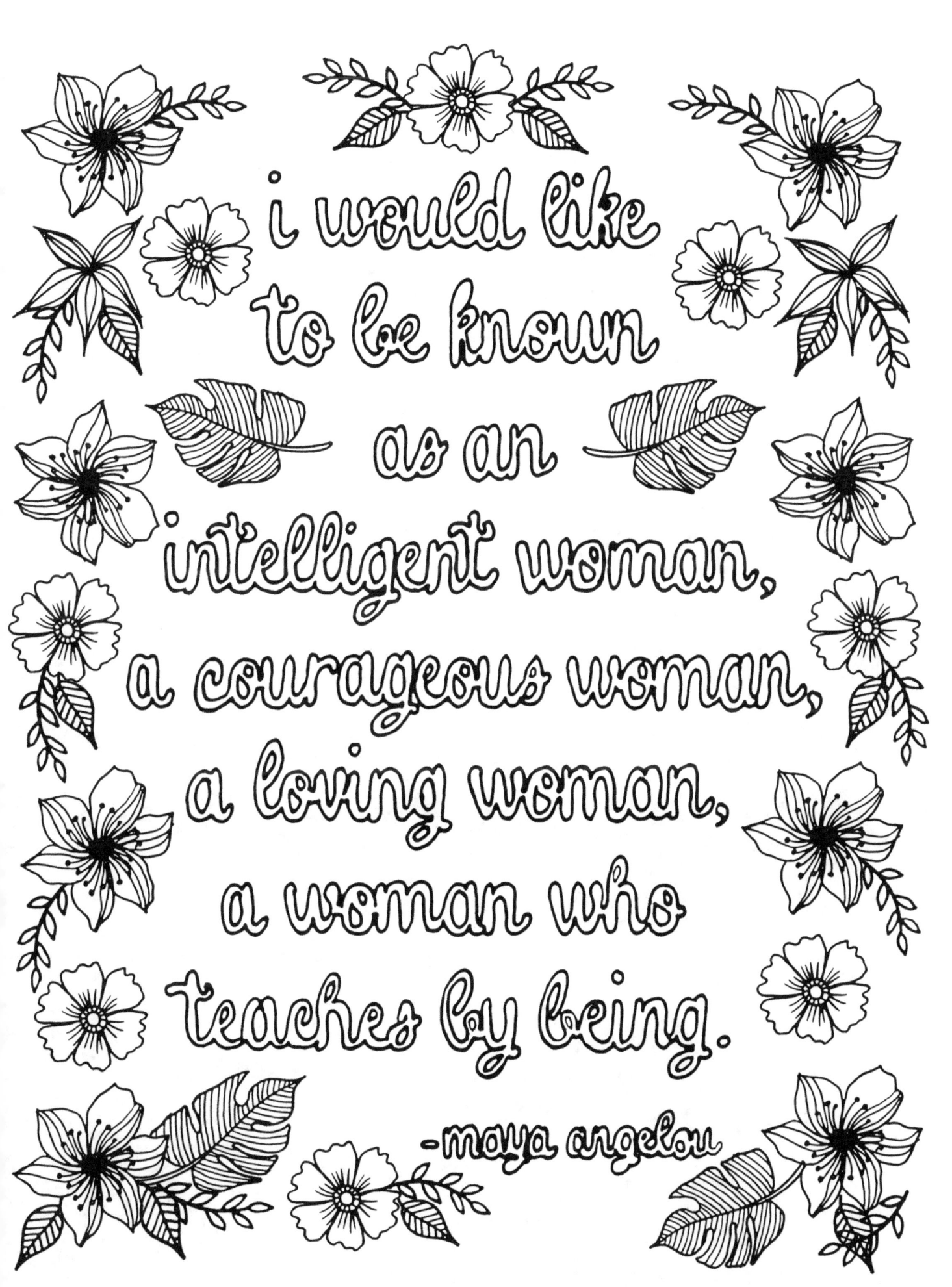

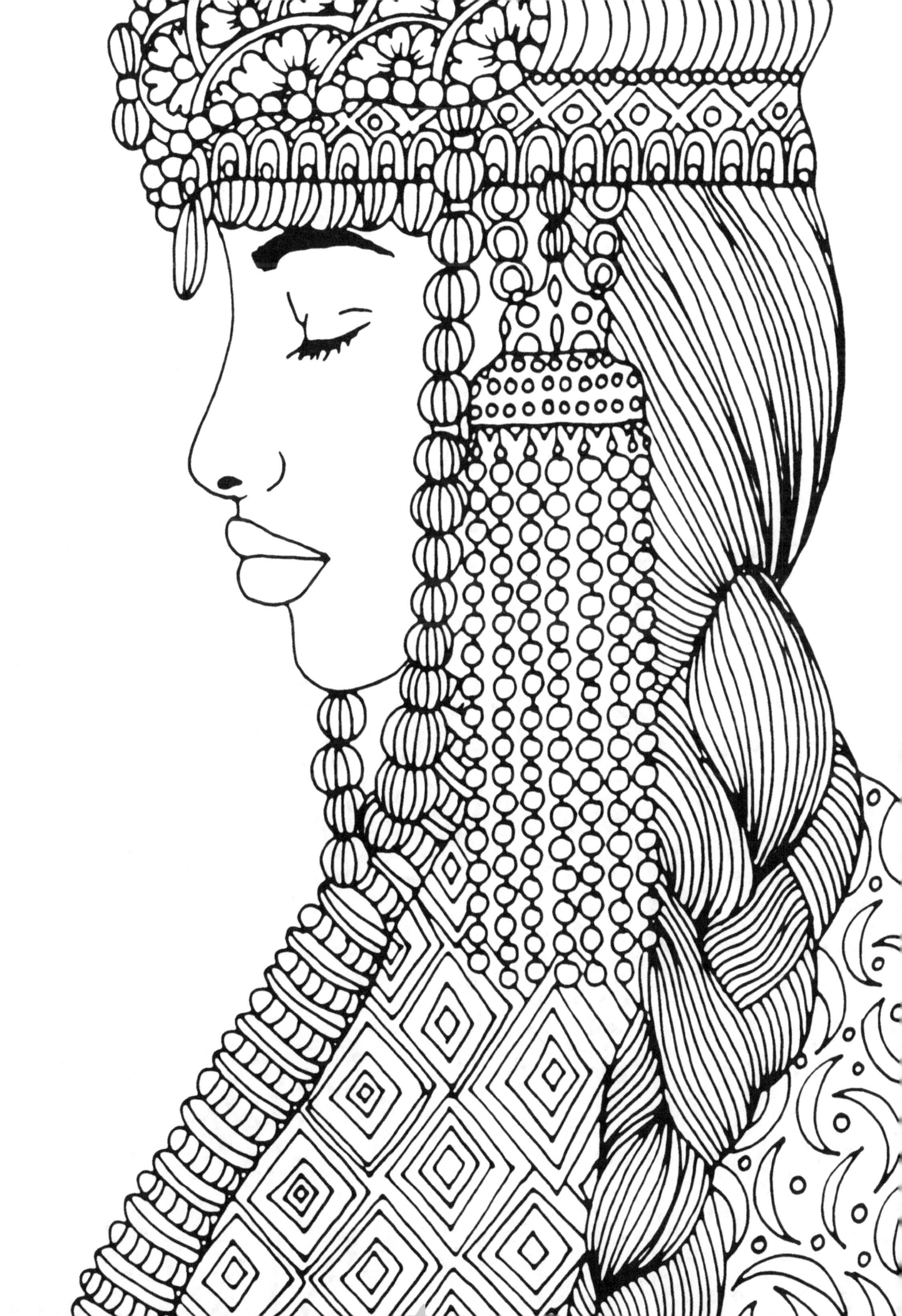

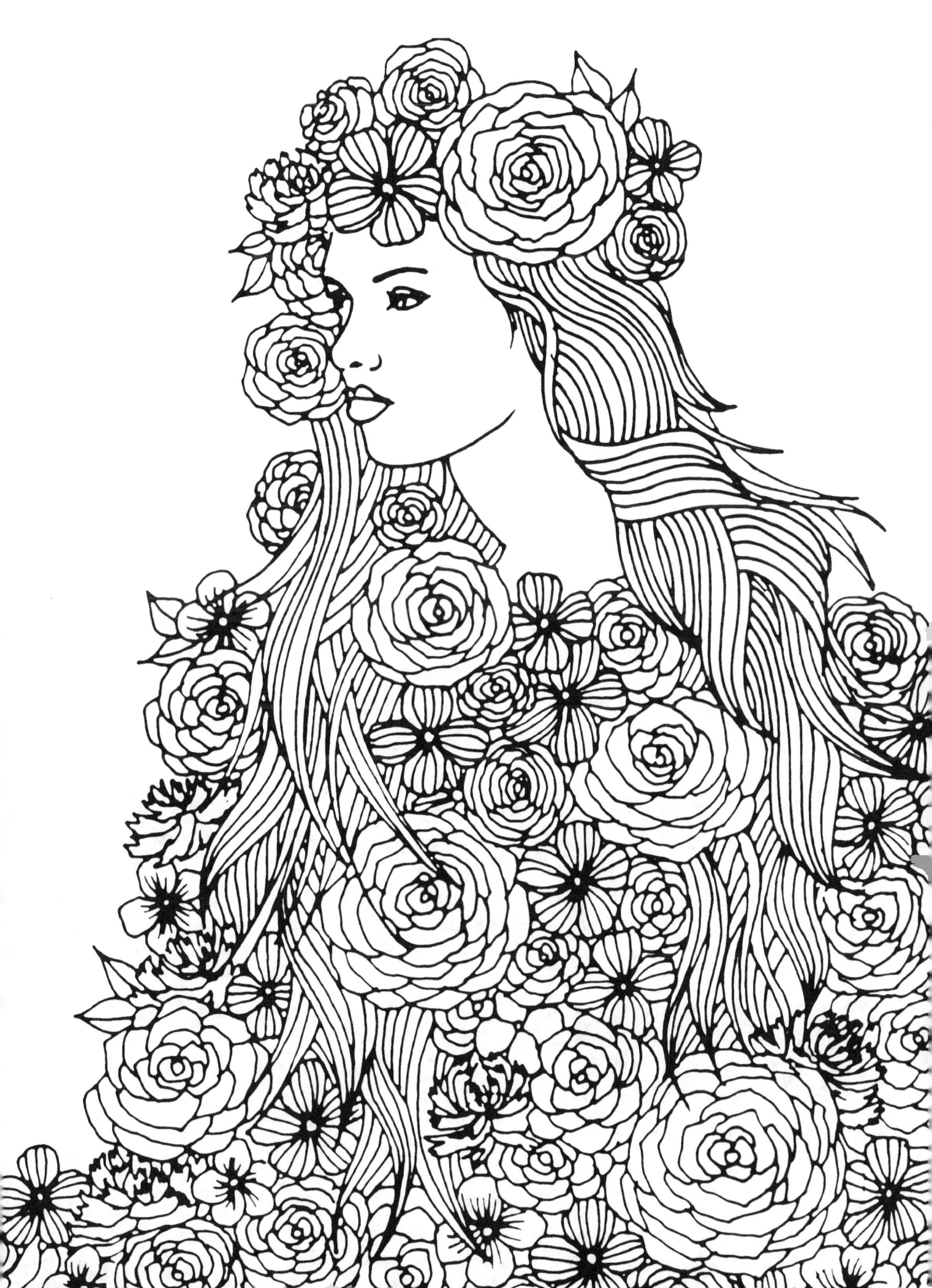

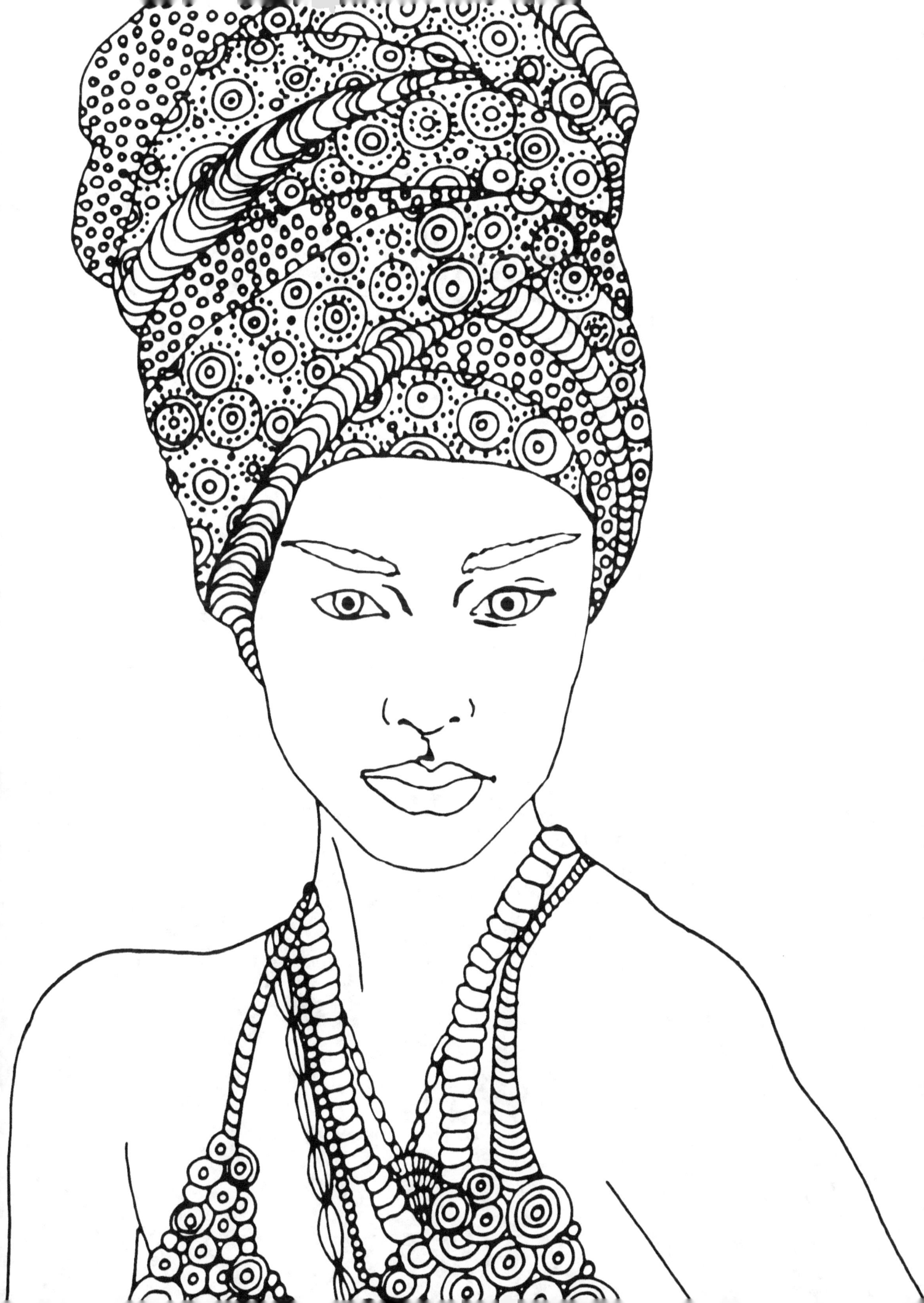

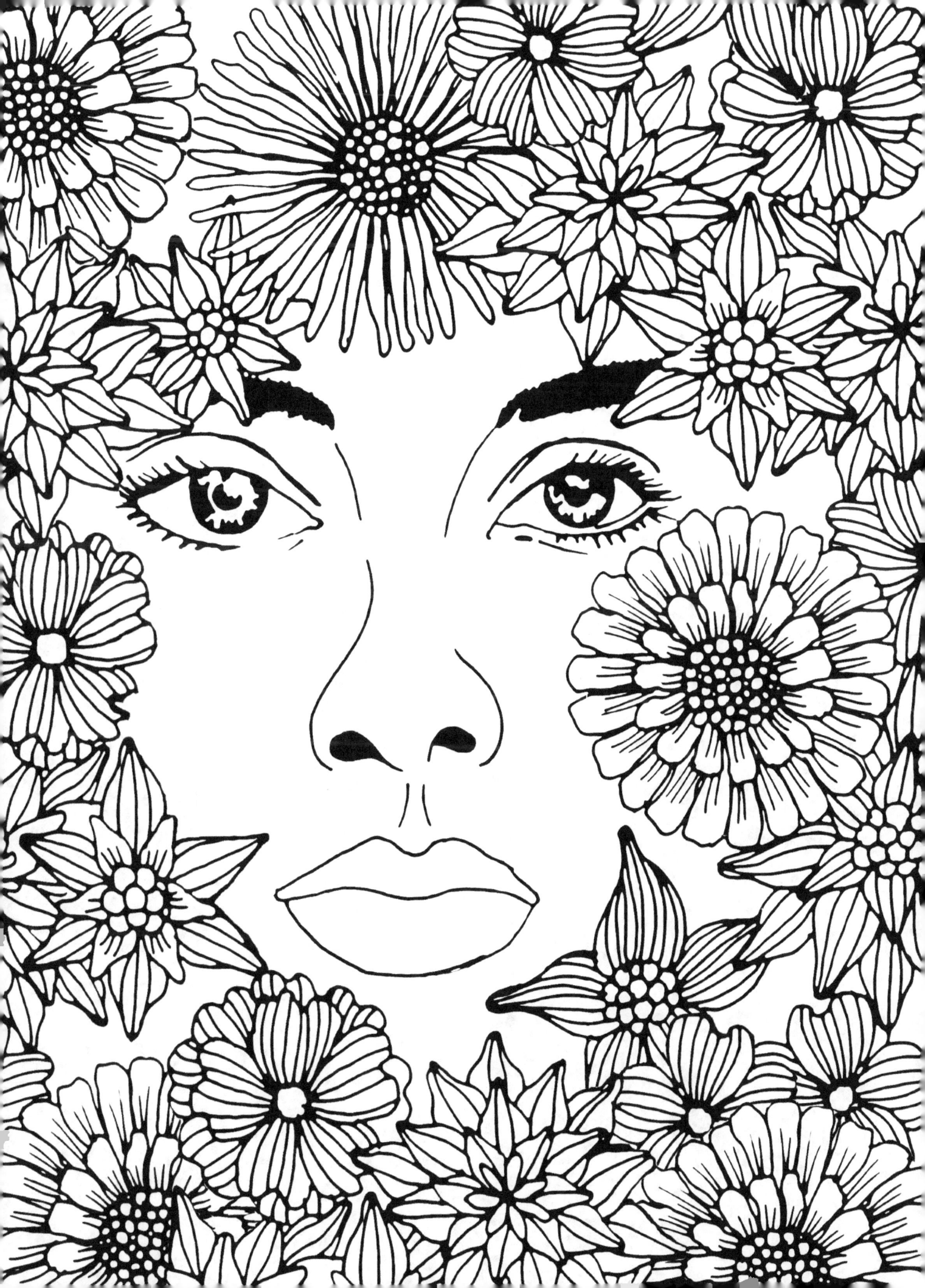

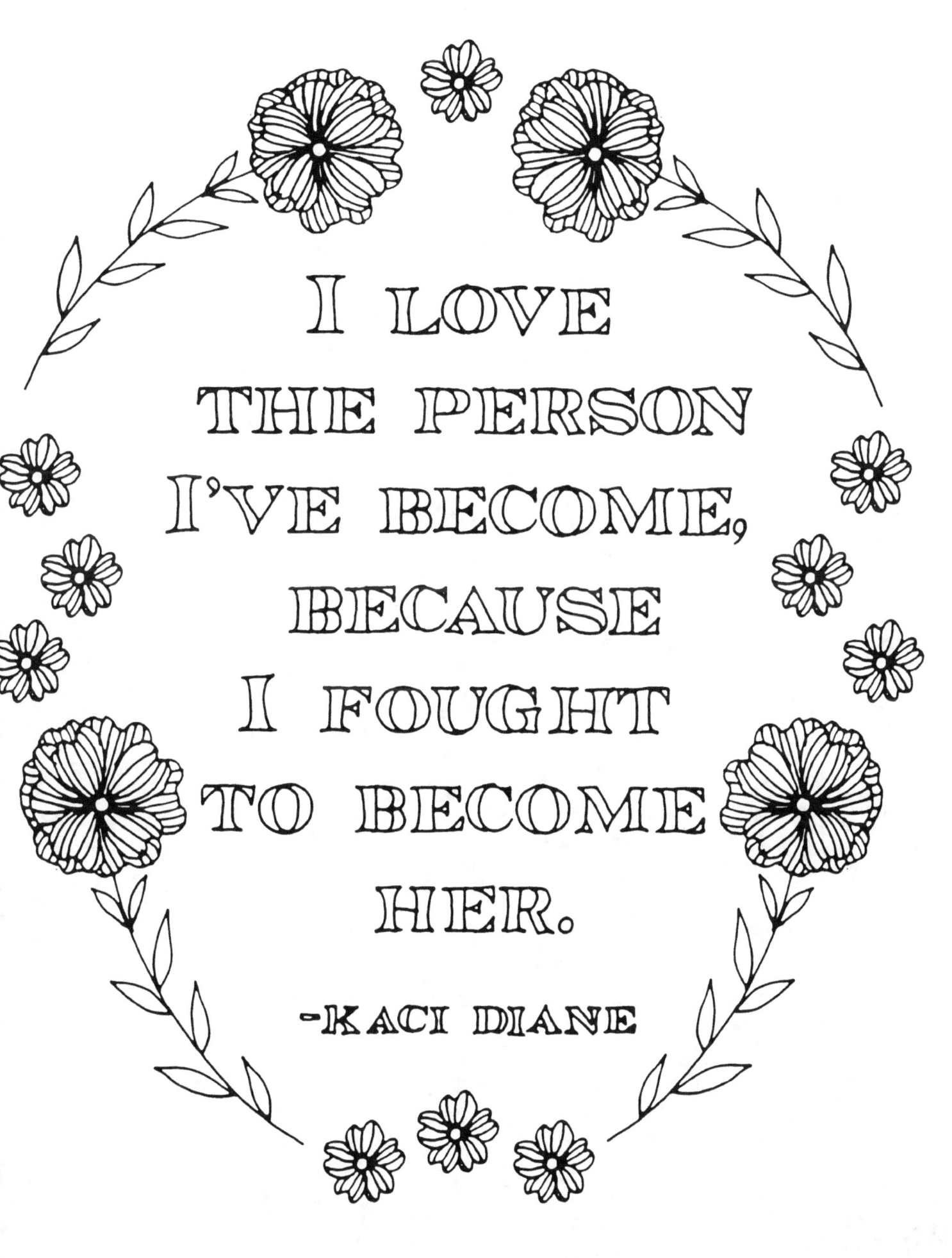

I LOVE
THE PERSON
I'VE BECOME,
BECAUSE
I FOUGHT
TO BECOME
HER.

-KACI DIANE